UNREACHED

What Every Educator Wants to Know About Engaging Families for Equity & Student Achievement

by Trise Moore

1641 Worthington Road, Suite 210
West Palm Beach, FL 33401
724.459.2100
email: pub@learningsciences.com
learningsciences.com

22 21 20 19 18   1 2 3 4 5

Names: Moore, Trise, author. Title: Unreached
Description: West Palm Beach, FL : Learning Sciences, 2019.
Identifiers: ISBN 978-1-943920-76-1 (paperback)
Subjects: LCSH: Education. | Literacy. | Effective teaching. | BISAC: EDUCATION / Professional Development. | EDUCATION / Aims & Objectives.

TABLE OF CONTENTS

In my 20 years of service in K–12 education systems, I've never met an educator who said they did not want to be inspired or supported by their students' families. In practice, those I have met are people who fall into three camps: the teachers who thrive off community support and actively seek family engagement; the teachers who accommodate the few active parents they have every year; and the teachers who believe a family's role is to support the child at home, and they should leave school to the professionals. These last two groups avoid conversations with parents for fear of saying or doing the wrong thing and may believe the benefits of family engagement don't outweigh the work it takes to get there. I've been a classroom teacher, and I know the anxiety that can come with seeing *that parent's* phone number come up on caller ID. The expectations and requirements for teachers seem to increase every year, and those measurements aren't based on family engagement; the measurements prioritize test results. It is far easier to keep the focus narrowed in on the classroom and the curriculum, and designate everything else as outside our control and, therefore, not worth any portion of the limited time, resources, and energy allocated to support student achievement.

The truth is that family engagement does take work, from both the school and the community structures we reach out to. Partnering with our students' families isn't a passive process; it's based on choices we have to make every day and a major shift in the mental perspective we bring to every family interaction. The payoff, of course, is immeasurable. Most educators understand and respect the fact that their students are part of a family and larger community that knows them well. Nevertheless, once these children enter the school building, system priorities often render family knowledge, perspective, language, and culture nearly invisible. These institutional priorities demand that educators apply a keen focus on curriculum, academic rigor, and test scores as the most important factors for achieving desired student outcomes. The only way to combat this disregard is to have allies involved in student learning that can offer the insights and inspiration relevant to each student—someone who knows that Jamie isn't avoiding his reading work because he's goofing off but because he's in the middle of a book series and just got to the best part; someone who knows Amber isn't purposefully cheating by sharing her answers with other students but that she's the oldest of her siblings and is used to helping people out when they get stuck. There is no better ally for a student than their family.

Indeed, there is significant evidence that students with more involved families see greater academic achievement than students with less involved families (Mapp & Kuttner, 2013). In my years as an educator, I've seen this advantage written off time and time again. Far too many teachers believe that if parents want to be involved, they will involve themselves or, a far more revealing assumption, that families who care about their children's success will drive their own involvement, while those other families must not care much for their child's development. The damage that assumptions and implicit biases like these bring to the classroom is hard to overstate. We know that one of the significant indicators of student success is family engagement, so why would we relegate it to the "if it happens, it happens" category?

Although there is significant research linked to the connection between student motivation, academic success, and family engagement, such research is rarely included in teacher preparation programs or district-level professional development discussions. As a result, educators are forced to adopt family engagement practices that are based on school priorities and traditional communication methods that further isolate unengaged—what I call unreached—families and their children. I believe it is important to reframe the way we discuss family partnerships to include these terms because labeling a family "unengaged" or "uninvolved" puts the impetus on them. It is critical that we shift the language and understand these families are not unengaged. They are unreached. It is the responsibility of the school to drive student success, and it is therefore our responsibility to initiate efforts to reach out.

Unfortunately, in our current system educators are inclined to rely on tools like flyers, newsletters, and parent/teacher conferences to support their partnership and outreach attempts with families. These tools typically end up in the hands of a few well-connected families and do little to reach the rest of the community. With little time or funds allocated to collaboration or training focused on effective family partnerships, educators are at a loss for where and how to begin family and community engagement outside of the typical outreach plan. When it comes to gleaning the insight that families can bring to the student motivation, engagement, and achievement effort, educators have been given limited opportunities to learn and understand the "why," "what," or "how" of authentic outreach and engagement for effective family partnerships. As a result, teachers and school teams end up spending valuable time planning new or more events, only to find out that new or more does not necessarily mean better partnerships or improved student outcomes.

This workbook is designed to help educators become more aware of the unintended cost of missed opportunities for students and unreached families in education. It is also designed to support the development of practices that will have a positive impact on their connection with community structures in a way that promotes engagement and enhances equity and student achievement. This workbook will ask a lot of you. It requires self-reflection, real discussion with parents, and development of a genuine professional learning community with at least a few motivated colleagues. The payoff for completing it will be real, measurable improvements to the academic, social, and emotional development of every one of your students, and the satisfaction that you have learned from and reached families in a way that improves your connections to and outcomes for your students.

ACKNOWLEDGMENTS

I am always grateful to God for giving me family and friends who uplift, inspire, and have lovingly challenged me. I am especially thankful for my husband, who has always believed in, encouraged, and stood by me through 33 years of marriage, and for my two adult children who have inspired me to write this book; they have taught me what matters most when it comes to family engagement. I also want to acknowledge and thank my brilliant sister-in-law and all of those who have graciously held me accountable as an educator and leader and kept me humble by forcing me to learn and grow beyond my comfort zone. I'm thankful for Dr. Mapp and other family engagement leaders who have worked tirelessly to provide the research that proves "family partnership" is really a legitimate thing that significantly supports student success. Thanks as well to Michele for coaching and reminding me about the tremendous value of one individual voice, whether it's my own or that of an individual parent who chooses to partner with his or her child's teacher.

Finally, thanks to each educator who wants to reach an unreached parent for a student's sake.

Always Sincerely,

Trise

ABOUT THE AUTHOR

Trise Moore received Education Week's 2017 national award for outstanding leadership in the area of family engagement, and she was identified as one of six "Emerging National Leaders" in the field of Family Engagement by Harvard's Family Research Project. She has designed and implemented community outreach and family engagement frameworks for districts and nonprofit organizations throughout the US. She has served on education advisory boards for the governor and presently serves on the Children and Youth Advisory Board for the King County Council, which represents one of the most diverse regions in the US. In 2010 she was named one of North West's Courageous Women of Power in Education by the North West Asian Weekly Foundation. She has taught on both the K–12 and higher-education levels and presently serves as a director of Equity and Family Engagement for one of the most diverse districts in the state of Washington. She has a master's degree in Program Management from City University and is presently working on her doctoral degree in Educational Leadership at City University of Seattle.

INTRODUCTION

To overcome our own implicit biases and more effectively incorporate students of culturally and socioeconomically diverse backgrounds into our classrooms, getting to know their community is an overlooked, but critical, step. Research indicates that family engagement has a greater impact on student academic success than race and income (Mapp & Kuttner, 2013). Other studies indicate that when educators know how to effectively incorporate a student's culture, community, and real-life examples into their lessons, it increases the chances of students becoming and staying engaged as learners (Hammond, 2015). John Hattie's research on student achievement and effect size identified teachers' perceptions, parental involvement, and students' beliefs about their performance as important factors contributing to positive student outcomes (Hattie, 2009). When teachers gain added insight, understanding, and support from families through effective partnerships, it can provide new and extensive opportunities to expand their perspective about students' abilities and, therefore, enhance their perception (Hammond, 2015). To close the achievement gap and increase student equity, engaging previously unreached families can be the single most effective change you make.

The goal of this workbook is to assist individual teachers, school teams, and building leaders as they collaborate with families to develop authentic, outcome-based approaches that support student achievement. This guide will assess where you are now; facilitate collaborative school, family, and community interactions for growth; and provide the structure necessary to organize and encourage continued engagement.

There are four partnership recommendations that lay the foundation for five leadership practices. Each of these recommendations is elaborated on in its own section, and you should freely move between sections as you identify particular areas of need. As an introduction, a brief summary of each follows.

The Four Equity Partnership Recommendations	
1. Earn Trust Early	**2. Share Responsibility Intentionally**
If trust is established early, families can more easily identify educators as allies and valuable partners. With a positive connection built on trust, families may also be more intentional about giving educators the benefit of the doubt when conflicts occur or when expectations need to be adjusted. Early encompasses initiating intentional and positive interactions regardless of the grade level (K–12, not just within the early grades).	When educators are intentional about becoming more familiar with the strengths-based assets, cultural norms, and knowledge that comes from students' families and community, sharing responsibility can become less complicated. Gaining purposeful clarity about when, how, and what to navigate as it pertains to partnership roles and activities can help prevent surprises and conflicts.
3. Balance Expectations Transparently	**4. Measure Efforts Meaningfully**
Constructing partnership goals openly and collectively (parent, teacher, student) can promote greater levels of clarity and help bring balance to spoken and unspoken expectations before conflicts arise. Transparent expectations also allow ideas and questions to be discussed in time for each party to reflect on and share their perspective about the boundaries that will help the partnership work most effectively.	Some data points and measures of success are less meaningful to parents than others and, although it's important to know what you're trying to accomplish for your students through your partnership efforts, it's also important to ask parents what their measurable and immeasurable hopes and goals are for their child/teenager. Your data priorities may not always match those of the families you serve but they can often be in alignment with and support your efforts.

The Five Authentic Leadership Practices	
1. Determine Student Outcomes	**2. Communicate Effectively**
Determine the student outcomes you want to accomplish with the support of your students' families.	Use parents' preferred communication methods whenever possible.
3. Recognize Cultural Assets and Norms	**4. Facilitate Collaborative Meetings**
Learn about students' cultural assets and norms by talking with families directly.	Cofacilitate parent meetings with codeveloped agenda topics.
5. Celebrate Together	
Share the stage and credit when celebrating progress.	

The structure of this guide will help you accomplish this goal through a series of reflection questions that follow each recommendation. The reflection questions are designed to introduce educators to concepts tied to the *what* and *how* of authentic family partnerships. After each reflection question, there is a typical scenario that describes how schools generally involve families—what you would see in a typical school with a typical community engagement plan.

As a quick note, you may recognize your own school's policies in these scenarios because these scenarios represent any school, in every state and city in the country. Identifying what areas you're putting energy and resources into and honestly evaluating their effectiveness in authentically reaching families, are critical components to this guide. Spending many hours designing a beautiful flyer can certainly take a lot of work, but is it the most effective way to use those hours? More effort doesn't necessarily mean more engagement, and many of the simplest measures for creating true family connections are overlooked. Working harder isn't the answer. What we want to do is work efficiently and authentically.

Following each of the recommendations, reflective questions, and typical scenarios are tips and strategies that have been developed from authentic classroom experience and family partnership research. They align with the five leadership practices and offer an extra layer of applicable relevance that helps familiarize educators with practical ways to apply the recommendations.

3

Your answers to the reflection questions are structured into response cards, which are not only valuable on an individual basis but also priceless when used collaboratively. There is space for both peer and parent contributions, and I cannot recommend the inclusion of these stakeholders from the beginning strongly enough. If you do not want to pass the book back and forth (although using it as a shared diary is certainly effective) or organize a series of collaborative meetings to complete it together, the response cards can be scanned and printed separately. You can also go deeper on a section or sections most pertinent to you by creating a jigsaw book study approach that allows you and your colleagues to exchange notes and ideas during grade-level, professional learning community, or professional development training sessions.

Although there are no cookie-cutter tools or approaches for partnership success, the four recommendations and five practices covered in this workbook, if implemented consistently and wholeheartedly, will permanently change the way your students are able to interact with their education. It isn't easy, and it will require you and the community with whom you interact to change some aspects of your relationship and expectations of each other. But all stakeholders have students' success and best interest at heart and this is the common ground we start from. By honoring families as valuable allies and advocates for their children, you will open the door to greater equity, higher engagement, and wider cultural experiences that enhance your professional growth and improve outcomes for every student forever.

Educators need to know that reaching families effectively requires time and a genuine interest in making connections that support meaningful conversations and trusting relationships, even more than research, strategies, or tips. When it comes to making these genuine connections, it's important to note that families, regardless of race, income, or education level, are a lot like educators in that they appreciate engaging and positive discussions that lead to productive outcomes. Take for example a time when you've been part of a rewarding group or an exciting solo project. You probably felt compelled to stay engaged and fully prepared to accept ownership of your part of the project until it was complete. What made that particular experience so engaging? What were the specific factors that initially motivated you and helped you stay motivated until you completed the project?

For most people, the factors surrounding their decision to engage involve common, personal descriptors, which can come in many forms, such as:

- ▶ *I had a passion for the project.*
- ▶ *When I shared my perspective, I felt heard.*
- ▶ *My opinion was respected and valued.*
- ▶ *I was confident that I had the skills needed to accomplish the task.*
- ▶ *I had a clear understanding of what it would take to accomplish the goal.*

In addition, they also state that they knew, trusted, or liked the people on the team and felt excited about the opportunity to be part of something meaningful and rewarding.

Review the motivation and engagement chart below. Designate a priority level for each of the factors listed, with 1 representing the factor with the highest level of importance to you as it pertains to making you want to engage in a project or partnership. Add any factors that are not listed as needed. After listing and selecting the factors that compel you to want to get and stay engaged, write a detailed explanation of what that particular factor would look like in practical and specific terms as it relates to that project from your perspective.

In spite of decades of educational initiatives and interventions, in the case of unreached families, few of these types of engagement factors have consistently existed for their children or teenagers. As a result, they may have little confidence that the experience will be different for them when they're invited to join conversations or attend school events. Typically, a school's attempts to communicate have been more like opportunities for parents to sit, listen, buy in and take notes rather than participate in an engaging exchange of ideas or partnership discussions that build ownership and shared responsibility for student achievement.

As a result, families have had limited opportunities to see or experience educators as their authentic partners for equity and student achievement unless or until a problem arises. On some occasions they may have selected to attend an event and even participate in the discussion but only at the special request of someone in the school they know and genuinely trust. More often than not, families are just as unsure about how to start the

Your Motivation & Engagement Preferences		
Factors That Make Me Want to Engage in a Project or Partnership	Priority Ranking	Detailed Description
Having a passion for the project		**Example:** *I enjoy gardening and I have always had a green thumb, so when a friend of mine asked me to help her start a garden club group in our neighborhood, I was very interested because I could pick the meeting time and location, I could use my talents, and I could get to know more of my neighbors who share common interests.*
Feeling heard, respected, valued		**Example:** *Feeling heard, respected, and valued means not being interrupted or scrutinized and having at least one or two people in the room nod their head in agreement when I share my perspective.*
Having confidence in my ability to contribute to or accomplish the partnership goals and outcomes		
Having a clear understanding of the expectations and time commitment		
Having a reasonable level of familiarity, trust, or respect for those who will be involved in the project/activity		
Other important factor not listed above:		
Other important factor not listed above:		

partnership effort as educators; therefore, it behooves educators to take the first positive step early, otherwise their first connection with their students' families may require special skills or a high level of skill in the area of conflict navigation or resolution.

Look at the factors that you ranked highest in priority (first and second) in Your Motivation & Engagement Preferences chart on the previous page. How have you or do you encourage those feelings in the families you reach out to? Do these particular elements of engagement exist in the partnership discussions and meetings you invite parents to attend? If so, how do you know? If these elements are already part of your approach to partnering with families, how often or consistently do these elements occur before and after meetings and events?

It's very possible that some of your students' families may have more or different descriptors regarding what motivates and engages them, in particular as it pertains to what makes them feel heard, respected, and valued. Nevertheless, reflecting on what personally makes you feel supported and engaged provides a general starting point, a starting point that will help you identify and examine practical and effective ways to establish genuine and meaningful connections with families to promote student achievement.

Keep the motivation and engagement preferences and the descriptors you developed in mind as you begin Section 1 of this guide.

Section 1

EARN TRUST EARLY

Earn the trust of parents early and with a focus on developing a connection that demonstrates your respect for the ideas, assets, and insights families bring to the partnership. Reaching out to parents with a positive message early in the school year helps to build a positive foundation for meaningful interactions and conversations. If educators can extend an invitation and make an effort to earn trust early on, they are more likely to reduce the amount of time spent addressing conflicts with their students or families throughout the remainder of the school year. Families are typically willing to share responsibility for their child or teenager's academic success if they believe their contribution will be respected and will make a difference. Trust reinforces both respect and shared responsibility, and shared responsibility promotes a platform for reasonable and balanced expectations within the partnership. In most cases, it's as simple as asking parents to share their perspective and creating opportunities for discussions that go deeper than the general 15 to 20 minute parent/teacher conference discussion.

There is a lot to be said about the early learning movement that speaks to the value of engaging children and families during and prior to the preschool years, but for the purposes of this workbook, *earn trust early* refers to initiating conversations at the beginning of the school year before problems occur and regardless of the grade level. Whether it's preschool or high school, earning the trust of a parent goes a long way toward establishing a foundation for positive connections and authentically engaging partnerships.

Consider your school's practices in connection with each question and think about your answer with a lens toward the student whose families have not yet been reached. Read the *Typical Scenario* and the *Tips & Application Strategies* that follow the question, then write your own school's typical scenario, as well as any similarities you can identify. After summarizing your school's typical scenario, analyze its strengths and challenges.

Completing your self-reflection is only the first step; identify two parents and a colleague that will read your response, provide their own response, and help you brainstorm a potential solution that can enhance the strengths and address the challenges you have identified. Collect your potential solutions for Section 6, where you will complete *The Collective Brainstorm* section.

1 Have we intentionally asked our families and students to share their views regarding how we can establish effective family engagement and partnership practices?

Typical Scenario:

Our school leadership team met for several weeks to plan the school open house event for families. We wanted to make sure families had all of the information they needed to help their students succeed in our school. We also wanted families to feel welcome at the beginning of the school year because we know a positive start will set the tone for the rest of the year. We had a great turnout of families who we already knew and those who lived close to the school. We felt like we put a lot of time and energy into an event that produced the same lukewarm results we see every year.

Tips & Application Strategies:

Consider inviting a broader group of parents to be part of your planning meetings, as their ideas are most likely to resonate with other parents whose children also attend your school. They may also be able to offer insights regarding effective ways to increase interest and spread the word about the event. In addition to including parents on your planning team, think about asking parents throughout the school year about their ideas for next year's open house event. Ask parents what makes them feel welcome. Finally, make sure your open house event provides families with an opportunity to get everything done in one day and in one place, and include a variety of community-based partners and resources that support student learning and success. Invite library representatives so students and their families can get library cards and find out if local organizations will donate school supplies and appropriate items to give away to each family that attends.

Earn Trust Early Multilevel Response Card #1		AQ1
Response Level One: Your Response		
Our School's Scenario		
Our School's Similarities to the Typical Scenario		
Our School's Strengths and Challenges		
Response Level Two: Parent Response		
Our School's Scenario		
Our School's Similarities to the Typical Scenario		
Our School's Strengths and Challenges		

Response Level Three: Parent Response	
Our School's Scenario	
Our School's Similarities to the Typical Scenario	
Our School's Strengths and Challenges	
Response Level Four: Peer Response	
Our School's Scenario	
Our School's Similarities to the Typical Scenario	
Our School's Strengths and Challenges	

Response Level Five: Collective Brainstorm Response	
Potential ideas or solutions that can enhance the strengths and address the challenges you've previously identified.	
Have we intentionally asked our families and students to share their views regarding how we can establish effective family engagement and partnership practices?	
Which of the following 5 Practices is already covered in our school's scenario? ■ Determine student outcomes ■ Recognize cultural assets and norms ■ Facilitate collaborative meetings ■ Communicate effectively ■ Celebrate together	
Which of the 5 Practices should be added as part of the brainstorm solution for this scenario?	
How can these missing practices be added, and how can the current practices be implemented more effectively?	

2

In what ways do our school practices, protocols, and events help with the process of building trust as it pertains to honoring student and family voice?

Typical Scenario:

It always seems that the closer we get to the end of the school year, the harder it gets to have honest conversations with parents about their student's progress. We try explaining to parents that they should attend student conferences and ask their students about their progress more often. No matter how often we remind parents to periodically check their child's progress, we still end up having conflicts in the middle and end of the year regarding their concerns that their child is not performing up to par.

Tips & Application Strategies:

Think about front-loading conversations and offer support recommendations sooner rather than later. Parents will be less inclined to feel frustrated or helpless about their child's lack of progress if they can take ownership of the solution in time to make a difference. In addition, find out if your school's parent notification system has the capability to send progress updates via auto call messaging, letters, texts, and/or grading software system alerts to families before students fall behind.

Earn Trust Early Multilevel Response Card #2	
Response Level One: Your Response	
Our School's Scenario	
Our School's Similarities to the Typical Scenario	
Our School's Strengths and Challenges	
Response Level Two: Parent Response	
Our School's Scenario	
Our School's Similarities to the Typical Scenario	
Our School's Strengths and Challenges	

Response Level Three: Parent Response	
Our School's Scenario	
Our School's Similarities to the Typical Scenario	
Our School's Strengths and Challenges	
Response Level Four: Peer Response	
Our School's Scenario	
Our School's Similarities to the Typical Scenario	
Our School's Strengths and Challenges	

Response Level Five: Collective Brainstorm Response *Potential ideas or solutions that can enhance the strengths and address the challenges you've previously identified.*	
Have we intentionally asked our families and students: Do our school protocols and events honor student and family voices and help with the process of building trust?	
Which of the following 5 Practices is already covered in our school's scenario? ■ Determine student outcomes ■ Recognize cultural assets and norms ■ Facilitate collaborative meetings ■ Communicate effectively ■ Celebrate together	
Which of the 5 Practices should be added as part of the brainstorm solution for this scenario?	
How can these missing practices be added, and how can the current practices be implemented more effectively?	

3

In what ways do our schools practices, protocols, and events create barriers to the process of building trust and honoring student and parent voices and partnerships?

Typical Scenario:

Our elementary and secondary schools have welcome signs posted at the front entrance in a variety of languages. On the elementary school level, we greet parents in the parking lot when they drop off their children in the morning. On the secondary school level, we have staff who greet students as they are getting off the bus and entering the school.

Tips & Application Strategies:

In addition to warm greeters and welcome signs, make sure all other signs posted outside of and in the building also have a welcoming tone. Most school signs feature "don't," "can't," "shouldn't," "must," or "caution" terminology, which can undo the positive feelings created by the warm greetings and welcome signs. Consider asking a variety of parents if they can take turns serving as volunteer greeters during various times of the school day to help make sure parents know where to sign in and how to find what they're looking for. Parents can also help other parents find out how to get the information and support they need to help their students. These volunteers can also be part of the school's parent leadership or advisory team, help establish a multicultural PTA group, or they may choose not to be part of either of those groups and just help the school feel more welcoming to families who have not previously felt connected to the school. Reaching out to a variety of parents who reflect the student population and making it easy for them to serve as volunteer greeters for short time frames that work in their schedule will increase the likelihood of parents volunteering in this capacity. More specifically, if you personally let parents know they are needed to help other families feel welcome, and simplify the time commitment so it can be as brief as one hour, once a month or two hours twice a year, parents will go out of their way to arrange their schedule so they can be at their child's school to serve in this capacity. In particular, since this volunteer assignment does not require a lengthy time commitment or extensive training and it has clear parameters, it is more appealing to parents who would like to get involved but whose schedules may not be that flexible.

Earn Trust Early Multilevel Response Card #3

Response Level One: Your Response	
Our School's Scenario	
Our School's Similarities to the Typical Scenario	
Our School's Strengths and Challenges	
Response Level Two: Parent Response	
Our School's Scenario	
Our School's Similarities to the Typical Scenario	
Our School's Strengths and Challenges	

Response Level Three: Parent Response	
Our School's Scenario	
Our School's Similarities to the Typical Scenario	
Our School's Strengths and Challenges	
Response Level Four: Peer Response	
Our School's Scenario	
Our School's Similarities to the Typical Scenario	
Our School's Strengths and Challenges	

Response Level Five: Collective Brainstorm Response *Potential ideas or solutions that can enhance the strengths and address the challenges you've previously identified.*	
Have we intentionally asked our families if there are any practices, protocols, or events that create barriers to the process of building trust and honoring student and family voices?	
Which of the following 5 Practices is already covered in our school's scenario? ■ Determine student outcomes ■ Recognize cultural assets and norms ■ Facilitate collaborative meetings ■ Communicate effectively ■ Celebrate together	
Which of the 5 Practices should be added as part of the brainstorm solution for this scenario?	
How can these missing practices be added, and how can the current practices be implemented more effectively?	

4

How can we glean parents' knowledge to help us understand our student's strengths, interests, and culture in a way that enhances partnerships and student engagement?

Typical Scenario:

The number of students in each class increases every year, almost as consistently as the expectations for improved outcomes. Despite these realities, we ask parents to share information with us about their child's or teenager's strengths, interests, and culture, but it seems that the parents who share this information are the parents whose children are already doing well.

Tips & Application Strategies:

Although some may wonder which came first, high performing students or highly engaged families, this pattern is another indication of a strong correlation between engaged families and successful students. Make it easy for more parents to contribute this type of information about their child or teenager by creating a fun and personally meaningful homework assignment for students that involve their parent(s). Have each student select three caring adults they know (e.g., family member, mentor, local community leader, neighbor), and encourage them to write the following questions on three different index cards:

I've been given a homework assignment that requires me to select and interview three different adults who can answer these three questions about me:

1. What strength(s) have you noticed about me?
2. What do you appreciate most about me?
3. What advice would you give me to help me achieve my goals and dreams?

Have the students fill in the answers they receive on each index card and provide time in class for each student to read the information from one of the interviews in front of the class. For students who prefer not to share in public, have them write a one- to two-page overview explaining what, if anything, they have in common with the individuals they selected and how they decided to pick the people they chose for the homework assignment. Have each student turn in each of their index cards so you can learn about the student's strengths, goals, and cultural context from a variety of perspectives.

Students will likely select three people they trust, identify with, or know well, which may include people who know their culture, strengths, and interests. Ask the student if they would like to invite one or all of the individuals to any of the events or partnership activities that occur throughout the school year.

Earn Trust Early Multilevel Response Card #4	
Response Level One: Your Response	
Our School's Scenario	
Our School's Similarities to the Typical Scenario	
Our School's Strengths and Challenges	
Response Level Two: Parent Response	
Our School's Scenario	
Our School's Similarities to the Typical Scenario	
Our School's Strengths and Challenges	

Response Level Three: Parent Response	
Our School's Scenario	
Our School's Similarities to the Typical Scenario	
Our School's Strengths and Challenges	
Response Level Four: Peer Response	
Our School's Scenario	
Our School's Similarities to the Typical Scenario	
Our School's Strengths and Challenges	

Response Level Five: Collective Brainstorm Response	
Potential ideas or solutions that can enhance the strengths and address the challenges you've previously identified.	
Have we intentionally asked our families how we can learn more about their child's interests, strengths, and culture in a way that enhances partnerships and student engagement?	
Which of the following 5 Practices is already covered in our school's scenario? ■ Determine student outcomes ■ Recognize cultural assets and norms ■ Facilitate collaborative meetings ■ Communicate effectively ■ Celebrate together	
Which of the 5 Practices should be added as part of the brainstorm solution for this scenario?	
How can these missing practices be added, and how can the current practices be implemented more effectively?	

When we use student and family feedback to improve our school culture and instructional practice, how do we let students and families know?

Typical Scenario:

We share information about school updates and changes with our PTA members during their meetings, and they spread the word with parents they know. We also have student representatives share information with students who participate in a variety of school-based clubs.

Tips & Application Strategies:

In addition to sharing updates and information with PTA and student leaders within the school, consider identifying parent and student representatives who don't participate in school leadership activities to help spread the word. Expand your outreach contact list to trusted apartment managers, childcare program managers and after-school program managers in your school neighborhood, as well as leaders of cultural associations and organizations that reflect your student population. Sharing information with a broad variety of members in the community will help ensure information in school updates reaches a broad variety of families.

Also consider making intentional efforts to identify and partner with leaders within your local community who represent the cultures of your students and families. These efforts will allow you to reach families who have not previously been reached, help you spread the word about school updates, and provide the connections you'll need when issues of greater importance need to be shared.

Earn Trust Early Multilevel Response Card #5	
Response Level One: Your Response	
Our School's Scenario	
Our School's Similarities to the Typical Scenario	
Our School's Strengths and Challenges	
Response Level Two: Parent Response	
Our School's Scenario	
Our School's Similarities to the Typical Scenario	
Our School's Strengths and Challenges	

Response Level Three: Parent Response	
Our School's Scenario	
Our School's Similarities to the Typical Scenario	
Our School's Strengths and Challenges	
Response Level Four: Peer Response	
Our School's Scenario	
Our School's Similarities to the Typical Scenario	
Our School's Strengths and Challenges	

Response Level Five: Collective Brainstorm Response	
Potential ideas or solutions that can enhance the strengths and address the challenges you've previously identified.	
Have we intentionally asked our families how we can use student and family feedback to improve our school culture and instructional practice, and how we should let them know when we do?	
Which of the following 5 Practices is already covered in our school's scenario? ■ Determine student outcomes ■ Recognize cultural assets and norms ■ Facilitate collaborative meetings ■ Communicate effectively ■ Celebrate together	
Which of the 5 Practices should be added as part of the brainstorm solution for this scenario?	
How can these missing practices be added, and how can the current practices be implemented more effectively?	

Recommendation Summary for School Teams:

Discuss each of the five questions covered in this section from a team perspective and include parents in the conversation. After completing answers to the questions as a team, move forward on the following recommendations:

- Decide how you will establish a Collaborative Family Engagement Team with a focus on how the team will help the school build trust early with a focus on equity and student achievement.

- Decide how you will make sure the team includes building leadership, parents, and representatives from a variety of grade levels, learning support categories, and cultural perspectives.

- Decide how you will work on each question as a group with a focus on developing one or two schoolwide strategies that will help the school improve its reach with unreached families.

- Decide how you will identify the desired objectives for the strategy, a specific start date, key roles for each team member, and how and when you will monitor progress toward the objective.

- Decide how you will revise schoolwide policies and practices so that they align with the desired objectives connected to reaching families who have not yet been reached for equity and student achievement.

Section 2

SHARE RESPONSIBILITY
INTENTIONALLY

Both families and educators alike are willing to take responsibility for what is needed to help a child or teenager succeed academically. However, it's likely that neither thinks about describing or identifying their part of the responsibility until they are directly asked, and even then, it's only somewhat intentional. As a result, assumptions are made about what shared responsibility looks like and clarity is only provided when and if things get complicated.

When educators are intentional about becoming more familiar with the strengths-based assets, cultural norms, and knowledge that comes from students' families and community, sharing responsibility can become less complicated. Gaining purposeful clarity about when, how, and what to navigate as it pertains to partnership roles and activities can help prevent surprises and conflicts.

Intentionally seeking and utilizing the family's knowledge, norms, and assets can help inform school practices regarding existing but untapped resources and support options. It can also promote shared responsibility because it increases and improves opportunities to include families in decision-making, leadership, and volunteer opportunities.

Consider your school's practices in connection with each question and think about your answer with a lens toward the student whose families have not yet been reached. Read the *Typical Scenario* and the *Tips & Application Strategies* that follow the question, then write your own school's typical scenario, as well as any similarities you can identify. After summarizing your school's typical scenario, analyze its strengths and challenges.

Completing your self-reflection is only the first step; identify two parents and a colleague who will read your response, provide their own response, and help you brainstorm a potential solution that can enhance the strengths and address the challenges you have identified. Collect your potential solutions for Section 6, where you will complete *The Collective Brainstorm* section.

1

What do parents want us to know about their family norms and their vision of "shared responsibility" as it pertains to supporting their child's success in school?

Typical Scenario:

We know that our families have more to share with us about their culture than the food they eat and clothing they wear, so during our multicultural events we also offer opportunities for families from various cultural groups to set up space in the school to share stories and historical facts with other families.

We invite community partners and respected cultural leaders in our community to facilitate the conversations in the library, the cafeteria, and in classrooms.

Tips & Application Strategies:

In some cases, parents are happy to fulfill their priority responsibilities at home and give their child's or teenager's teachers the courtesy of managing all things school related. This approach can reflect a respect for the teacher, a belief that their child can do well regardless, a hectic schedule, and/or a lack of confidence in their capacity to make a difference. These are just a few of the possible reasons why educators have not been able to reach more families in the effort to promote equity and student achievement.

For the most part, schools have offered parents very few reasons to believe that their cultural norms and vision of shared responsibility would be honored or valued. Without long-standing trust and a genuine and clear invitation to these types of opportunities, it becomes unlikely that parents will automatically accept a request to share this type of information. Even in cases where trust has been built early and expectations of shared responsibility have been established, we have to take into account power and privilege factors. If parents are willing to become vulnerable enough to share their cultural norms and their vision of shared responsibility, what happens if educators and decision makers judge their vision and norms to be insignificant? There are few tips or strategies for answering a question of this level of complexity, so the best way to find an answer is to make sure you're ready for the discussion.

Share Responsibility Intentionally Multilevel Response Card #1	
Response Level One: Your Response	
Our School's Scenario	
Our School's Similarities to the Typical Scenario	
Our School's Strengths and Challenges	
Response Level Two: Parent Response	
Our School's Scenario	
Our School's Similarities to the Typical Scenario	
Our School's Strengths and Challenges	

Response Level Three: Parent Response	
Our School's Scenario	
Our School's Similarities to the Typical Scenario	
Our School's Strengths and Challenges	
Response Level Four: Peer Response	
Our School's Scenario	
Our School's Similarities to the Typical Scenario	
Our School's Strengths and Challenges	

Response Level Five: Collective Brainstorm Response *Potential ideas or solutions that can enhance the strengths and address the challenges you've previously identified.*	
Have we intentionally asked our families what they want us to know about their family norms and vision for shared responsibility as they support their child's success in school?	
Which of the following 5 Practices is already covered in our school's scenario? ■ Determine student outcomes ■ Recognize cultural assets and norms ■ Facilitate collaborative meetings ■ Communicate effectively ■ Celebrate together	
Which of the 5 Practices should be added as part of the brainstorm solution for this scenario?	
How can these missing practices be added, and how can the current practices be implemented more effectively?	

2 In what ways can we use family insight to inform our prevention, intervention, and school improvement planning?

Typical Scenario:

One of my colleagues mentioned that her student's dad stumbled on an effective way to help his son focus on his schoolwork after playing outside. The idea was easy to implement, so my colleague tried it with the student one day after he returned from recess. The idea worked and my colleague called and told the dad and he thanked her and told her that she is the first teacher who ever asked him for his ideas for how to prevent his son from getting overwhelmed or how to calm him down when he does.

Tips & Application Strategies:

If only the work of intervention and prevention could always be that simple. We all know that student engagement and motivation are much more complicated than the sample scenario would lead us to believe. Nevertheless, some scenarios end up being much more complicated than necessary because we include parents as the last resort for identifying effective resources and options linked to student engagement, motivation, or achievement.

Share Responsibility Intentionally Multilevel Response Card #2	
Response Level One: Your Response	
Our School's Scenario	
Our School's Similarities to the Typical Scenario	
Our School's Strengths and Challenges	
Response Level Two: Parent Response	
Our School's Scenario	
Our School's Similarities to the Typical Scenario	
Our School's Strengths and Challenges	

Response Level Three: Parent Response	
Our School's Scenario	
Our School's Similarities to the Typical Scenario	
Our School's Strengths and Challenges	
Response Level Four: Peer Response	
Our School's Scenario	
Our School's Similarities to the Typical Scenario	
Our School's Strengths and Challenges	

Response Level Five: Collective Brainstorm Response *Potential ideas or solutions that can enhance the strengths and address the challenges you've previously identified.*	
Have we intentionally asked our families what insights they have about ways we can address intervention and prevention steps for their student?	
Which of the following 5 Practices is already covered in our school's scenario? ■ Determine student outcomes ■ Recognize cultural assets and norms ■ Facilitate collaborative meetings ■ Communicate effectively ■ Celebrate together	
Which of the 5 Practices should be added as part of the brainstorm solution for this scenario?	
How can these missing practices be added, and how can the current practices be implemented more effectively?	

3 What type of academic resources, assignments, or opportunities do we share with students and families to help make the most of out-of-school learning opportunities?

Typical Scenario:

During holiday breaks, I've asked my students to practice their writing skills by writing a short story or journaling over the break. To increase their motivation, I've offered to let them use what they've written over the break in place of one of their class assignments.

Tips & Application Strategies:

Give students a specific writing prompt that encourages them to pick a topic that is connected to a family tradition or career goal and invite them to include their family or someone they admire in the community as a proofreader or collaborator. Reach out to each student's family or have the student notify their family before the break starts to let them know about the assignment so they can be prepared to participate.

Share Responsibility Intentionally Multilevel Response Card #3	
Response Level One: Your Response	
Our School's Scenario	
Our School's Similarities to the Typical Scenario	
Our School's Strengths and Challenges	
Response Level Two: Parent Response	
Our School's Scenario	
Our School's Similarities to the Typical Scenario	
Our School's Strengths and Challenges	

Response Level Three: Parent Response	
Our School's Scenario	
Our School's Similarities to the Typical Scenario	
Our School's Strengths and Challenges	

Response Level Four: Peer Response	
Our School's Scenario	
Our School's Similarities to the Typical Scenario	
Our School's Strengths and Challenges	

Response Level Five: Collective Brainstorm Response	
Potential ideas or solutions that can enhance the strengths and address the challenges you've previously identified.	
Have we intentionally asked our families what types of academic resources and opportunities would they find helpful as they support their students' learning during holidays and summer breaks?	
Which of the following 5 Practices is already covered in our school's scenario? ■ Determine student outcomes ■ Recognize cultural assets and norms ■ Facilitate collaborative meetings ■ Communicate effectively ■ Celebrate together	
Which of the 5 Practices should be added as part of the brainstorm solution for this scenario?	
How can these missing practices be added, and how can the current practices be implemented more effectively?	

4 What are some ways we can honor and learn more about the assets and cultural norms our students and families bring?

Typical Scenario:

Our school staff has discussions about equity and culture during the appropriately designated times of the year. During these dates, we invite guest speakers who represent a variety of cultures and backgrounds to give presentations in class and during school assemblies.

Tips & Application Strategies:

Periodic discussions and activities linked to equity and culture can, to some degree, offer an introduction to the assets and norms that students and families bring. In addition to honoring special dates celebrating various cultures, incorporate speakers and leaders who reflect your student population into school conversations year-round rather than just during annual cultural events. Invite these presenters to serve on panels and during professional development sessions. Have your professional development planning team work with the speakers to set up question and answer sessions and/or ask the speakers to share their expertise in connection with the cultural norms and community assets they would like to discuss with staff.

Share Responsibility Intentionally Multilevel Response Card #4	
Response Level One: Your Response	
Our School's Scenario	
Our School's Similarities to the Typical Scenario	
Our School's Strengths and Challenges	
Response Level Two: Parent Response	
Our School's Scenario	
Our School's Similarities to the Typical Scenario	
Our School's Strengths and Challenges	

Response Level Three: Parent Response	
Our School's Scenario	
Our School's Similarities to the Typical Scenario	
Our School's Strengths and Challenges	

Response Level Four: Peer Response	
Our School's Scenario	
Our School's Similarities to the Typical Scenario	
Our School's Strengths and Challenges	

Response Level Five: Collective Brainstorm Response *Potential ideas or solutions that can enhance the strengths and address the challenges you've previously identified.*	
Have we intentionally asked our families how we can honor and learn more about the cultural norms and assets your family wants us to know about?	
Which of the following 5 Practices is already covered in our school's scenario? ■ Determine student outcomes ■ Recognize cultural assets and norms ■ Facilitate collaborative meetings ■ Communicate effectively ■ Celebrate together	
Which of the 5 Practices should be added as part of the brainstorm solution for this scenario?	
How can these missing practices be added, and how can the current practices be implemented more effectively?	

5 How can we invite families to help us incorporate cultural relevance and equity within the district, school, and classroom levels?

Typical Scenario:

Our school has a multicultural event each year that encourages families and students to wear clothing and share food and artifacts from their country of origin. We let students create art and projects that represent their culture and help them create posters and displays.

Tips & Application Strategies:

Try any of the suggestions in the *Typical Scenario* above and also incorporate opportunities for students to write about professional or famous leaders from their culture who have excelled in careers or achievements that match those they aspire to accomplish. Encourage students to collaborate with their families to find or create videos, short essays, or poems that share a positive message connected to something about their culture.

Share Responsibility Intentionally Multilevel Response Card #5	
Response Level One: Your Response	
Our School's Scenario	
Our School's Similarities to the Typical Scenario	
Our School's Strengths and Challenges	
Response Level Two: Parent Response	
Our School's Scenario	
Our School's Similarities to the Typical Scenario	
Our School's Strengths and Challenges	

Response Level Three: Parent Response	
Our School's Scenario	
Our School's Similarities to the Typical Scenario	
Our School's Strengths and Challenges	
Response Level Four: Peer Response	
Our School's Scenario	
Our School's Similarities to the Typical Scenario	
Our School's Strengths and Challenges	

Response Level Five: Collective Brainstorm Response *Potential ideas or solutions that can enhance the strengths and address the challenges you've previously identified.*	
Have we intentionally asked our families how we can incorporate cultural relevance and equity within the district, school, and classroom levels?	
Which of the following 5 Practices is already covered in our school's scenario? ■ Determine student outcomes ■ Recognize cultural assets and norms ■ Facilitate collaborative meetings ■ Communicate effectively ■ Celebrate together	
Which of the 5 Practices should be added as part of the brainstorm solution for this scenario?	
How can these missing practices be added, and how can the current practices be implemented more effectively?	

Recommendation Summary for School Teams:

Discuss each of the five questions in this section from a team perspective and include parents in the conversation. After completing answers to the questions as a team, move forward on the following recommendations:

- Decide how you will connect in like groups (e.g., staff with staff, parents with parents, students with students) to discuss what shared responsibility means to each group as it pertains to engaging in partnerships to promote equity and student achievement.

- Decide how you will collaborate around each group's perspective regarding what shared responsibility means to them and identify areas of commonality.

- Decide how you will capture two or three concepts or ideas that each group had in common and work collectively to develop shared agreements and shared meaning on how to support and promote those shared agreements.

- Decide how you will identify the desired objectives for the strategy, a specific start date, key roles for each team member, and how and when you will monitor progress toward the objective.

- Decide how you will revise schoolwide policies and practices so that they align with the desired objectives connected to reaching families that have not yet been reached for equity and student achievement.

Section 3

BALANCE EXPECTATIONS TRANSPARENTLY

Educators and families usually have incredibly high expectations for themselves and each other, so much so that both can feel overwhelmed when the student is not succeeding. Constructing partnership goals collectively (parent, teacher, and student) can promote greater levels of clarity and help bring balance to spoken and unspoken expectations before conflicts arise. Having conversations that allow a transparent, two-way exchange of ideas and expectations between families and educators gives the student an opportunity to see, hear and understand what is expected of him or her. It can also generate positive intentions focused on how each member of the partnership can and will support the student's success.

Making positive connections that inform and highlight first and next steps for each partner, promotes transparency. If each person in the partnership openly and in advance specifies their hopes and expectations, it can help avoid unreasonable requests down the road when and if the student needs extra support. Starting the partnership off with an understanding of the level of effort each person can contribute prevents the need to adjust and recalibrate as a result of a misunderstanding.

Consider your school's practices in connection with each question and think about your answer with a lens toward the student whose families have not yet been reached. Read the *Typical Scenario* and the *Tips & Application Strategies* that follow the question, then write your own school's typical scenario, as well as any similarities you can identify. After summarizing your school's typical scenario, analyze its strengths and challenges.

Completing your self-reflection is only the first step; identify two parents and a colleague who will read your response, provide their own response, and help you brainstorm a potential solution that can enhance the strengths and address the challenges you have identified. Collect your potential solutions for Section 6, where you will complete *The Collective Brainstorm* section.

1 When and how do we ask our families about their expectations for their student's progress and their views about their role in their student's progress?

Typical Scenario:

We reach out to families through parent surveys and during evening events to find out how they want to be involved in the school, but we continue to get the same families and the same information each time. We also ask them at the beginning of the year during open house events, and we take note of their comments so we can revisit them as we prepare for parent/teacher conferences.

Tips & Application Strategies:

Be explicit about your interest in learning from families, make it easy for them to tell you, and ask more than once. Parent surveys can be effective if the surveys are short, easy to use, and are offered both in electronic and hard-copy formats for parents who don't have access to technology. When and if parents believe that you really want to know and that you will do something with the information when you get it, then they are eager to share their perspective. After you've received responses, be sure to share the results and how you will apply them to make improvements. To further reinforce your desire to build trust and measure efforts meaningfully, ask parents for their input on how to analyze and make meaning of the survey results. Use their input to make improvements and let them know how and when through a variety of their preferred communication channels. Provide specific ideas and opportunities with regard to ways they can be involved in next steps on the school or district level and ask them to help you create or improve family partnership practices.

Balance Expectations Transparently Multilevel Response Card #1	
Response Level One: Your Response	
Our School's Scenario	
Our School's Similarities to the Typical Scenario	
Our School's Strengths and Challenges	
Response Level Two: Parent Response	
Our School's Scenario	
Our School's Similarities to the Typical Scenario	
Our School's Strengths and Challenges	

Response Level Three: Parent Response	
Our School's Scenario	
Our School's Similarities to the Typical Scenario	
Our School's Strengths and Challenges	
Response Level Four: Peer Response	
Our School's Scenario	
Our School's Similarities to the Typical Scenario	
Our School's Strengths and Challenges	

Response Level Five: Collective Brainstorm Response *Potential ideas or solutions that can enhance the strengths and address the challenges you've previously identified.*	
Have we intentionally asked our families what their expectations are about their student's progress and their role is in that progress?	
Which of the following 5 Practices is already covered in our school's scenario? ■ Determine student outcomes ■ Recognize cultural assets and norms ■ Facilitate collaborative meetings ■ Communicate effectively ■ Celebrate together	
Which of the 5 Practices should be added as part of the brainstorm solution for this scenario?	
How can these missing practices be added, and how can the current practices be implemented more effectively?	

2 In what ways do we address limited technology access, language, transportation, childcare, and scheduling constraints when we invite families to partner?

Typical Scenario:

Our principal gives us the option to schedule our biannual parent–teacher and student conferences in teams at the apartment cabana where our students and families live. This approach addresses the transportation barriers that often exist for our students and their families.

Taking the event to families rather than always expecting families to come to the school is a good first step toward addressing some of the barriers to establishing an effective partnership with families.

Tips & Application Strategies:

It may also be a good idea to select a location that has technology access and invite interpreters and childcare providers to be part of the team and meetings. These considerations can make the meeting more productive in cases where families speak a different language and have children who need to be supervised during the meeting. Ask parents what locations and time of day works best for scheduling meetings and consider staggering staff participation so a morning and evening meeting option can be offered whenever possible. If meeting times coincide with meal times provide a light but appropriate meal to both staff and families.

Balance Expectations Transparently Multilevel Response Card #2	
Response Level One: Your Response	
Our School's Scenario	
Our School's Similarities to the Typical Scenario	
Our School's Strengths and Challenges	
Response Level Two: Parent Response	
Our School's Scenario	
Our School's Similarities to the Typical Scenario	
Our School's Strengths and Challenges	

Response Level Three: Parent Response	
Our School's Scenario	
Our School's Similarities to the Typical Scenario	
Our School's Strengths and Challenges	
Response Level Four: Peer Response	
Our School's Scenario	
Our School's Similarities to the Typical Scenario	
Our School's Strengths and Challenges	

Response Level Five: Collective Brainstorm Response *Potential ideas or solutions that can enhance the strengths and address the challenges you've previously identified.*	
Have we intentionally asked our families what prevents them from participating in school activities and partnering with school staff?	
Which of the following 5 Practices is already covered in our school's scenario? ■ Determine student outcomes ■ Recognize cultural assets and norms ■ Facilitate collaborative meetings ■ Communicate effectively ■ Celebrate together	
Which of the 5 Practices should be added as part of the brainstorm solution for this scenario?	
How can these missing practices be added, and how can the current practices be implemented more effectively?	

3 Which parents respond positively to our partnership outreach efforts, and which parents seem less responsive and why?

Typical Scenario:

Some of my students' parents forget to sign forms that allow students access to technology, field trips, and after-school programs. We mailed the forms in the registration packets at the beginning of the school year, sent as attachments through email, and also sent them home with students. I'm unable to send individual reminders, so some of my students end up missing the opportunity.

Tips & Application Strategies:

Find out if there is another reason the parent may not be signing the forms. Consider possible religious and or cultural reasons the parents might have for choosing to have their child miss the activity or field trip. Also consider religious and cultural event dates that may conflict with school events or activities. Ask your students and/or families to help you review the school expectations, programs, and calendar with an equity lens. Connect with community groups and local organizations to find out if they can supplement or help your school make adjustments to the present school-based activities and program offerings.

Balance Expectations Transparently Multilevel Response Card #3	
Response Level One: Your Response	
Our School's Scenario	
Our School's Similarities to the Typical Scenario	
Our School's Strengths and Challenges	
Response Level Two: Parent Response	
Our School's Scenario	
Our School's Similarities to the Typical Scenario	
Our School's Strengths and Challenges	

Response Level Three: Parent Response	
Our School's Scenario	
Our School's Similarities to the Typical Scenario	
Our School's Strengths and Challenges	
Response Level Four: Peer Response	
Our School's Scenario	
Our School's Similarities to the Typical Scenario	
Our School's Strengths and Challenges	

Response Level Five: Collective Brainstorm Response *Potential ideas or solutions that can enhance the strengths and address the challenges you've previously identified.*	
Have we intentionally asked our families what type of outreach efforts work best for them?	
Which of the following 5 Practices is already covered in our school's scenario? ■ Determine student outcomes ■ Recognize cultural assets and norms ■ Facilitate collaborative meetings ■ Communicate effectively ■ Celebrate together	
Which of the 5 Practices should be added as part of the brainstorm solution for this scenario?	
How can these missing practices be added, and how can the current practices be implemented more effectively?	

4

How can you avoid burnout and manage your school responsibilities, family engagement efforts, and personal self-care with balance?

Typical Scenario:

As a building leader, between staff meetings and student activities, I often have three to four evening obligations a week. To make sure I don't burn out my staff, I schedule all meetings to start at 4:30 p.m. so they can be over by 6:00 or 6:30 p.m. so staff have time to be home with their own families.

Tips & Application Strategies:

Parents also prefer to avoid a lot of evening meetings after work. With this in mind, consider scheduling fewer meetings but make sure the start time coincides with parents' work schedules. Many parents work until 5 p.m. and contend with traffic on their way home to school events; scheduling meetings before they can arrive could discourage parents from participating. Reducing the number of events per week by making events multipurpose, conveniently scheduled, and meaningful for both staff and families will help ensure better turnout and less pressure on staff and families. Scheduling curriculum and math night on the same evening as the job fair or career day, for example, frees up two evenings and adds variety and convenience. The event may need to start earlier and end later, but it prevents the need to have three events on three separate evenings.

Balance Expectations Transparently Multilevel Response Card #4	
Response Level One: Your Response	
Our School's Scenario	
Our School's Similarities to the Typical Scenario	
Our School's Strengths and Challenges	
Response Level Two: Parent Response	
Our School's Scenario	
Our School's Similarities to the Typical Scenario	
Our School's Strengths and Challenges	

Response Level Three: Parent Response	
Our School's Scenario	
Our School's Similarities to the Typical Scenario	
Our School's Strengths and Challenges	
Response Level Four: Peer Response	
Our School's Scenario	
Our School's Similarities to the Typical Scenario	
Our School's Strengths and Challenges	

Response Level Five: Collective Brainstorm Response	
Potential ideas or solutions that can enhance the strengths and address the challenges you've previously identified.	
Have we intentionally asked ourselves how we can identify a scheduling compromise that works for staff, students, and our families, so that we can model our own healthy work/life balance?	
Which of the following 5 Practices is already covered in our school's scenario? ■ Determine student outcomes ■ Recognize cultural assets and norms ■ Facilitate collaborative meetings ■ Communicate effectively ■ Celebrate together	
Which of the 5 Practices should be added as part of the brainstorm solution for this scenario?	
How can these missing practices be added, and how can the current practices be implemented more effectively?	

5

What are some ways our families and community partners can provide direct support to the school community?

Typical Scenario:

We have discovered that not all of the community partners we invite to work with our families have been culturally responsive enough to help us promote trusting relationships. Consequently, we've learned to be transparent with our families and to ask them to be transparent with us about which community-based organizations truly honor their cultural norms and which seem less inclined to promote culturally responsive partnerships.

Tips & Application Strategies:

Ask parents to help you identify community partners that lead and serve with a lens toward engaging all families for equity and student achievement. If parents are unable to provide you with this type of information, have someone contact community organizations in your school and district and let them know your school/district policies and beliefs regarding engaging and serving all families and students for equity and student achievement. Last, ask them to provide information, evidence, or parent testimonials verifying the same.

Balance Expectations Transparently Multilevel Response Card #5	
Response Level One: Your Response	
Our School's Scenario	
Our School's Similarities to the Typical Scenario	
Our School's Strengths and Challenges	
Response Level Two: Parent Response	
Our School's Scenario	
Our School's Similarities to the Typical Scenario	
Our School's Strengths and Challenges	

Response Level Three: Parent Response	
Our School's Scenario	
Our School's Similarities to the Typical Scenario	
Our School's Strengths and Challenges	
Response Level Four: Peer Response	
Our School's Scenario	
Our School's Similarities to the Typical Scenario	
Our School's Strengths and Challenges	

Response Level Five: Collective Brainstorm Response *Potential ideas or solutions that can enhance the strengths* *and address the challenges you've previously identified.*	
Have we intentionally asked our families what are some ways our community partners can provide support, and who are the community partners who are most effective and culturally responsive from their perspective?	
Which of the following 5 Practices is already covered in our school's scenario? ■ Determine student outcomes ■ Recognize cultural assets and norms ■ Facilitate collaborative meetings ■ Communicate effectively ■ Celebrate together	
Which of the 5 Practices should be added as part of the brainstorm solution for this scenario?	
How can these missing practices be added, and how can the current practices be implemented more effectively?	

Recommendation Summary for School Teams:

Discuss each of the five questions in this section from a team perspective and include parents in the conversation. After completing answers to the questions as a team, move forward on the following recommendations:

- Decide how you will work as a group to summarize the expectations that will support effective outcomes with the shared responsibilities discussed in the previous section.

- Decide how you will generate mutually agreeable ideas for balancing those expectations as a team, in partnership with families.

- Decide how you will discuss ways to recognize misunderstandings linked to the expectations and how they will be managed to maintain positive intent.

- Decide how you will identify the desired objectives for the strategy, a specific start date, key roles for each team member and how and when you will monitor progress toward the objective.

- Decide how you will revise schoolwide policies and practices so that they align with the desired objectives connected to reaching families that have not yet been reached for equity and student achievement.

Section 4

MEASURE EFFORTS MEANINGFULLY

Some data points and measures of success are less meaningful to parents than others when it comes to developing effective family partnerships. Although it's important to know what you're trying to accomplish for your students through your partnership efforts, it's also important to ask parents what their measurable and immeasurable hopes and goals are for their child or teenager and to help them find ways to monitor and learn more about the data that aligns with those goals.

A meaningful measure might be how effectively they are able to identify ways to support and monitor their child's progress toward obtaining the credits and courses needed to get a scholarship for college. Finding out what matters most to the student and family in terms of the student's strengths and college and career goals can be very helpful. It can be even more helpful to the family and student if educators can refer them directly to the specific staff members, resources, community partners, or contacts that will help them make effective use and meaning of the data and college and career planning information that matters most to them. Although many parents are aware of some of the tools, data, and opportunities available through school services and resources, unreached parents are often unaware of the process required to utilize such services.

Consider your school's practices in connection with each question and think about your answer with a lens toward the student whose families have not yet been reached. Read the *Typical Scenario* and the *Tips & Application Strategies* that follow the question, then write your own school's typical scenario, as well as any similarities you can identify. After summarizing your school's typical scenario, analyze its strengths and challenges.

Completing your self-reflection is only the first step; identify two parents and a colleague who will read your response, provide their own response, and help you brainstorm a potential solution that can enhance the strengths and address the challenges you have identified. Collect your potential solutions for Section 6, where you will complete *The Collective Brainstorm* section.

1 What are some of the immeasurable benefits your students' families hope to gain from a partnership with you and/or their child's school?

Typical Scenario:

One of my students' parents was concerned about how to help her child manage the transition from elementary to middle school. She wanted my advice on ways she could support that transition without being overbearing. I helped the parent connect with other parents who were having similar apprehensions and put them in contact with a few of the staff members who work at the middle school where their child would be attending.

Tips & Application Strategies:

This is an example of an ideal way to offer a warm hand-off for students and families moving from elementary to secondary school level. Another approach might include providing a schoolwide event at the elementary, middle, and high schools for all students and families who will be facing this type of transition. Inviting students, families, and community partners to participate in a schoolwide or districtwide event with a focus on transitions is something that many schools and districts have been doing for years. However, some of these events focus more on providing paperwork and information. The most helpful transition events are those that provide the required paperwork, as well as resource connections with community partners, and opportunities for parents and students to have conversations with staff.

Measure Efforts Meaningfully Multilevel Response Card #1	
Response Level One: Your Response	
Our School's Scenario	
Our School's Similarities to the Typical Scenario	
Our School's Strengths and Challenges	
Response Level Two: Parent Response	
Our School's Scenario	
Our School's Similarities to the Typical Scenario	
Our School's Strengths and Challenges	

Response Level Three: Parent Response	
Our School's Scenario	
Our School's Similarities to the Typical Scenario	
Our School's Strengths and Challenges	
Response Level Four: Peer Response	
Our School's Scenario	
Our School's Similarities to the Typical Scenario	
Our School's Strengths and Challenges	

Response Level Five: Collective Brainstorm Response *Potential ideas or solutions that can enhance the strengths and address the challenges you've previously identified.*	
Have we intentionally asked our families what are some of the benefits they're hoping to gain from our partnership?	
Which of the following 5 Practices is already covered in our school's scenario? • Determine student outcomes • Recognize cultural assets and norms • Facilitate collaborative meetings • Communicate effectively • Celebrate together	
Which of the 5 Practices should be added as part of the brainstorm solution for this scenario?	
How can these missing practices be added, and how can the current practices be implemented more effectively?	

2
What are the measurable outcomes you want to achieve for your students as a result of your partnership with their families?

Typical Scenario:

I wanted to increase the number of students who reach grade-level success in my math class, so I planned a math night event for parents. I sent out flyers a week in advance and posted all of the event information on the school website and only six parents showed up.

Tips & Application Strategies:

Parents rarely check school websites unless and until they are looking for something specific. Unless your school has an app that pushes event or flyer notifications directly to their phone via text or email, it's unlikely that they will notice or find your announcements. Flyers are great if they are posted on or near spots common to families' everyday activities (e.g., school bus drop-off locations, the front door of the school, library, grocery store, fitness center, apartment cabana) Families will feel more compelled to attend if they receive a personal invitation from a staff member or parent they know. It's also a good idea to give parents two to three weeks' notice and notify them in a variety of ways more than once.

Although it's a small number, six parents attending your math night event means six students will have parents with a clearer understanding of how to help them in math. It will make a difference for those six students.

Measure Efforts Meaningfully Multilevel Response Card #2	
Response Level One: Your Response	
Our School's Scenario	
Our School's Similarities to the Typical Scenario	
Our School's Strengths and Challenges	
Response Level Two: Parent Response	
Our School's Scenario	
Our School's Similarities to the Typical Scenario	
Our School's Strengths and Challenges	

Response Level Three: Parent Response	
Our School's Scenario	
Our School's Similarities to the Typical Scenario	
Our School's Strengths and Challenges	
Response Level Four: Peer Response	
Our School's Scenario	
Our School's Similarities to the Typical Scenario	
Our School's Strengths and Challenges	

Response Level Five: Collective Brainstorm Response *Potential ideas or solutions that can enhance the strengths and address the challenges you've previously identified.*	
Have we intentionally asked ourselves what outcomes we want to achieve for our students as a result of our partnership with their families?	
Which of the following 5 Practices is already covered in our school's scenario? • Determine student outcomes • Recognize cultural assets and norms • Facilitate collaborative meetings • Communicate effectively • Celebrate together	
Which of the 5 Practices should be added as part of the brainstorm solution for this scenario?	
How can these missing practices be added, and how can the current practices be implemented more effectively?	

3 What are some of the effective family partnership activities other schools and districts use to produce measurable outcomes for student achievement?

Typical Scenario:

Every year our district sends a team to a state or national family engagement conference to learn about what other schools and districts are doing. We take school teams that consist of parents, teachers from each grade level, a building leader, and some district administrators.

Tips & Application Strategies:

Learning from others who have had success is an excellent way to learn something new and build on prior knowledge without reinventing the wheel. Nevertheless, it is sometimes difficult to find funding for travel, and staff members are usually weary of workshop warriors when they come back from trainings like these. Given this scenario, make sure to share ideas that offer quick wins and are easy to implement.

In addition, be intentional about making time to regroup as a team to identify which specific ideas will work well in your local school or district. Also, be sure to collaborate as a team around your new learnings and identify what your measurable objectives and next steps might look like before springing all of the new ideas on the folks back home.

Measure Efforts Meaningfully Multilevel Response Card #3	
Response Level One: Your Response	
Our School's Scenario	
Our School's Similarities to the Typical Scenario	
Our School's Strengths and Challenges	
Response Level Two: Parent Response	
Our School's Scenario	
Our School's Similarities to the Typical Scenario	
Our School's Strengths and Challenges	

Response Level Three: Parent Response	
Our School's Scenario	
Our School's Similarities to the Typical Scenario	
Our School's Strengths and Challenges	
Response Level Four: Peer Response	
Our School's Scenario	
Our School's Similarities to the Typical Scenario	
Our School's Strengths and Challenges	

Response Level Five: Collective Brainstorm Response *Potential ideas or solutions that can enhance the strengths and address the challenges you've previously identified.*	
Have we intentionally asked ourselves what other schools and/or districts are doing in partnership with families to produce positive and measurable outcomes for student success?	
Which of the following 5 Practices is already covered in our school's scenario? ■ Determine student outcomes ■ Recognize cultural assets and norms ■ Facilitate collaborative meetings ■ Communicate effectively ■ Celebrate together	
Which of the 5 Practices should be added as part of the brainstorm solution for this scenario?	
How can these missing practices be added, and how can the current practices be implemented more effectively?	

4 How can I build on my expanded understanding of effective partnership approaches to enhance my leadership skills and professional goals?

Typical Scenario:

I incorporate my partnership work with my students' families to enhance my list of skills and experience on my résumé and as evidence in my evaluation summary.

Tips & Application Strategies:

Find out if your building leader or district offers stipends for staff members who create trainings or facilitate discussions on the topic of family engagement and partnerships. Use this workbook to introduce the recommendations to teachers in your school or on the district level as a continuous learning class for clock hour credits.

Measure Efforts Meaningfully Multilevel Response Card #4	
Response Level One: Your Response	
Our School's Scenario	
Our School's Similarities to the Typical Scenario	
Our School's Strengths and Challenges	
Response Level Two: Parent Response	
Our School's Scenario	
Our School's Similarities to the Typical Scenario	
Our School's Strengths and Challenges	

Response Level Three: Parent Response	
Our School's Scenario	
Our School's Similarities to the Typical Scenario	
Our School's Strengths and Challenges	
Response Level Four: Peer Response	
Our School's Scenario	
Our School's Similarities to the Typical Scenario	
Our School's Strengths and Challenges	

Response Level Five: Collective Brainstorm Response	
Potential ideas or solutions that can enhance the strengths and address the challenges you've previously identified.	
Have we intentionally asked ourselves how we can build on our expanded understanding of effective partnership approaches to enhance our individual and collective leadership skills and professional goals?	
Which of the following 5 Practices is already covered in our school's scenario? ■ Determine student outcomes ■ Recognize cultural assets and norms ■ Facilitate collaborative meetings ■ Communicate effectively ■ Celebrate together	
Which of the 5 Practices should be added as part of the brainstorm solution for this scenario?	
How can these missing practices be added, and how can the current practices be implemented more effectively?	

5 How can families help us measure our progress toward the goal of reaching families for equity and student achievement?

Typical Scenario:

Most of our teachers live outside of the school community and have long commutes to and from work, so they prefer to limit the number of evening meetings they attend after school. However, they are very interested in learning about the broader school community and cultural norms of their students and families, but they aren't sure where or how to start. We have a variety of school events, but we're hoping to find a way to build on to the events we already have scheduled within the school year in a way that expands our knowledge and understanding of the community and students we serve.

Tips & Application Strategies:

Work with families and community partners to coordinate a multipurpose event (e.g., open house, back-to-school event, parent–teacher conference events, transition planning night) and select a location outside of the school (e.g., community center, apartment cabana, library). Include time on the meeting agenda for families to share their knowledge about the community and community partners they trust. School staff can provide information about academic support strategies that can be used at home, and students and parents can talk about the student's interests and strengths. Display student work and have community organizations, cultural clubs, and after-school programs bring resources and set-up booths. The objective of the event would be to increase staff knowledge about their students and the community, as well as glean parent knowledge that can be used to improve the school climate and culture to increase student engagement levels. A specific progress measure would be the number of students whose parents are aware of programs and supports for their children and the number of children that get signed up for activities/programs that will increase their engagement levels in experiences that promote learning. A specific staff-related progress measure would be the number of teachers who feel more aware of, connected to, and confident about using the resources and assets surrounding their school community.

In addition to those measurable indicators, include parents and (high school) students in the discussion about the outcomes they believe to be most important and how they can help the school meet the objectives linked to those outcomes.

Measure Efforts Meaningfully Multilevel Response Card #5

Response Level One: Your Response	
Our School's Scenario	
Our School's Similarities to the Typical Scenario	
Our School's Strengths and Challenges	
Response Level Two: Parent Response	
Our School's Scenario	
Our School's Similarities to the Typical Scenario	
Our School's Strengths and Challenges	

Response Level Three: Parent Response	
Our School's Scenario	
Our School's Similarities to the Typical Scenario	
Our School's Strengths and Challenges	
Response Level Four: Peer Response	
Our School's Scenario	
Our School's Similarities to the Typical Scenario	
Our School's Strengths and Challenges	

Response Level Five: Collective Brainstorm Response
Potential ideas or solutions that can enhance the strengths and address the challenges you've previously identified.

Have we intentionally asked our families if they can help us identify ways to measure our progress toward the goal of achieving effective family partnerships that support equity and student achievement?	
Which of the following 5 Practices is already covered in our school's scenario? • Determine student outcomes • Recognize cultural assets and norms • Facilitate collaborative meetings • Communicate effectively • Celebrate together	
Which of the 5 Practices should be added as part of the brainstorm solution for this scenario?	
How can these missing practices be added, and how can the current practices be implemented more effectively?	

Recommendation Summary for School Teams:

Discuss each of the five questions in this section from a team perspective and include parents in the conversation. After completing answers to the questions as a team, move forward on the following recommendations:

- Decide how you will ask your families to share their perspective on the most effective ways to connect and partner with them to increase student engagement and achievement efforts.

- Decide how you will work with families to help you identify and accomplish a specific, quantifiable goal that will enhance the school's family partnership efforts with a specific outcome focused on student achievement.

- Decide how you will determine the resources, tools, timelines, and key roles needed to accomplish the desired outcomes as well as how and when you will monitor progress toward the objective.

- Decide how you will identify the desired objectives for the strategy, a specific start date, key roles for each team member, and how and when you will monitor progress toward the objective.

- Decide how you will revise schoolwide policies and practices so that they align with the desired objectives connected to reaching families who have not yet been reached for equity and student achievement.

Section 5

THE FIVE AUTHENTIC PARTNERSHIP PRACTICES

When implemented under the umbrella of the four equity and partnership recommendations, the five authentic partnership practices offer more specific and comprehensive insight around the details needed to develop an approach that ensures equity and effective reach to all of your students' families.

Determine Student Outcomes

Determine what you want to accomplish for your students as a result of the partnership with their families (e.g., improve student attendance, advance reading level, identify the student's strengths and interests, discover hidden talent that can be used to enhance student motivation, increase understanding for how to use the student's cultural assets and family traditions in a way that supports learning, get the student to read and practice class lessons at home and turn in assignments, adjust prevention and intervention strategies) and ask parents for their help, feedback, or ideas.

Recognize Cultural Assets and Norms

Be willing to learn insights directly from your students' families and trusted community leaders as it pertains to their cultural assets and norms rather than just share what you want them to do or know. Consider the fact that students and their families represent a broad variety of experiences, knowledge, and perspectives. Your students and their families also represent community assets that influence, enhance, support, and define student performance. Acknowledging these factors will help you gain insight that can inform and improve your practice and partnerships with families. It can also help make the instructional strategies you use to improve student engagement levels more relevant.

Facilitate Collaborative Meetings

Design parent meetings so that the agendas are codeveloped with parents and meetings are cofacilitated by parents. Parents are less interested in presentations when the agenda is crafted and delivered by staff only. Ask parents what type of agenda topics matter most to them and encourage them to help lead or be part of the meeting presentation. Including parents in these ways helps ensure a greater level of interest, ownership, relevance, and participation.

Communicate Effectively

Ask parents their top three preferred methods for receiving information and opportunities connected to school activities and their child's progress, and use those methods as often as possible. Aligning communication efforts with approaches that meet the needs of families can prevent the extra work that comes with missed messages and misunderstandings. Finding practical ways to exchange ideas and share information effectively increases the chances of families developing the level of trust required to establish effective partnerships.

Celebrate Together

Look for and create opportunities to share the spotlight, give credit, and celebrate progress with families and their children as often as possible at the school and in the community. When parents become part of the solution and celebration, it builds positive momentum for their student, the school, and their partnership with staff. Including families in activities that honor their contribution reinforces trust and supports meaningful connections.

The Authentic Partnership Self-Assessment

Reflect on the questions in the Authentic Partnership Self-Assessment chart that follows. Answer the questions and identify the response that matches you and/or your school's partnership approach in connection with each statement. After selecting the response that indicates where you believe you or your school's present approach fits, place an X next to any or all of the descriptors that you or your school will include in your new and improved approach.

Authentic Partnership Self-Assessment Chart				
Equity & Partnership Reflection Questions				
	Always	Sometimes	Not Yet	New Approach
I initiate positive connections with my students' families early so that I can build trust and partner with an equity lens for student achievement.				
I know the specific learning and partnership outcomes I would like families to help me accomplish with and for all of my students.				
I know how to effectively engage and partner with all of my students' families to support the learning outcomes we all want to accomplish for their children/teenagers.				

I ask all families to share their knowledge with me regarding their children/ teenagers' strengths, interests, and cultural assets.			
I use the information families share about their children/ teenagers to inform my instructional practice and help me enhance student engagement and learning.			
I ask my students' families what they think I should know and what they want to know from me before planning parent activities and meetings.			

I include parents and also encourage my colleagues and building leader to include parents in decision-making meetings that will impact their students.				
I brainstorm and help implement ideas with parents to help develop improvements related to a variety of topics focused on equity and access for students and families.				
I know and frequently use the top two methods of communication preferred by my students' families when sharing information about their progress or partnership opportunities.				

I let parents know how their partnership has made a difference in their students' success as a learner and in my role as an educator.				
I include families in presentations and celebration efforts linked to promoting and honoring their partnership and student progress.				

After completing the Self-Assessment chart, identify how many and which of the items in the assessment you will include and prioritize in your improved and authentic approach in Section 6 of the workbook. You may want to include two or three items from both the "Sometimes" and "Not Yet" categories as you complete the chart in Section 6.

Section 6

Your Plan

Lessons Learned

Every time an educator makes an effort to engage with a student's family in support of that student's success—even if it doesn't yield the desired result—a valuable lesson can be learned. This section offers a short list of lessons learned, within the context of the Four Equity Partnership Recommendations. Review the insights offered in the 'Lesson' column and pay special attention to the two columns that follow the 'Lesson' column, as they may provide new ideas and learnings you will want to add to your summary chart of next steps at the end of this section.

On occasion, some have confused increased attendance and involvement at school events as an indicator of effective family partnerships. When used effectively, the five authentic partnership practices provide a greater level of opportunity to develop effective family partnerships in that they help educators and schools capture the elements of the four recommendations with a lens toward reaching families that are often unreached.

Engaging families for equity and student achievement requires shared responsibility, shared effort, and shared respect, whereas parent involvement denotes an invitation to join an activity that has already been implemented or planned. Families can be reached more effectively if they genuinely believe their engagement can and will produce meaningful opportunities to build trust with staff and help their child or teenager succeed in school.

Families can be highly involved and even highly engaged, but if the same families participate every time or if they have not been part of the decision making for how they will have an impact on positive student outcomes, it isn't an effective partnership for equity and student achievement. After all of the work you have put into completing this workbook, hopefully this chart is a summary of the key takeaways on what reaching families is. . .and what it isn't.

The Four Equity Partnership Recommendations	Lesson . . .	Learned . . .	Consider reaching the families you haven't reached yet by:
Earn Trust Early	▪ Don't wait for parents to contact you first.	▪ Reaching out to parents with a positive message early in the school year can promote a positive foundation for partnerships and future conversations.	▪ Sending a positive message such as a postcard, leaving a voice message, or emailing the parents of your students who did not attend the open house or back-to-school night within the first three weeks of school
Share Responsibility Intentionally	▪ Everyone is willing to take responsibility for student achievement, but very few are clear about what shared responsibility looks like.	▪ Being intentional about when and how to navigate partnership roles and activities linked to student achievement helps prevent surprises and conflicts at the end of the school year.	▪ Becoming more familiar with the strengths-based assets, cultural norms, and knowledge that come from your students' families and community; intentionally utilizing these assets to inform school and instructional practice, decision-making, leadership, and volunteer opportunities

Balance Expectations Transparently	■ Educators and families have high expectations for themselves and each other, and both feel overwhelmed when the student is not succeeding.	■ Transparently co-constructing partnership goals collectively (parent, teacher, student) promotes greater levels of clarity and balance expectations when conflicts arise.	■ Making authentic connections that offer opportunities to have a transparent, two-way exchange of ideas and expectations between parent and teacher.
Measure Efforts Meaningfully	■ Some data points and measures of success are less meaningful than others when it comes to parent partnerships.	■ Ask parents what their measurable and immeasurable hopes and goals are for their child/teenager and help them identify ways to support and monitor that progress when possible.	■ Finding out what matters most to the student and family in terms of the student's strengths and college or career goals; referring them directly to the staff members, resources, community partners, and contacts who can help them make effective use and meaning of the data and college and career planning information that matters most to them.

Engaging Families for Equity & Student Achievement	
Is . . .	Isn't . . .
Identifying specific outcomes you want for your students and including parents in the discussion and efforts to achieve those outcomes.	Communicating information to families about what the school wants them to know and what they need to do.
Understanding how to glean and utilize parents' knowledge about cultural norms, students' strengths, and potential engagement strategies.	Requiring students and families to assimilate and align their beliefs and values with institutional practices that reinforce system protocols.
Parent meetings and events with topics and agendas that are codeveloped and cofacilitated by parents and educators.	A lot of events and meetings that provide entertainment and food.
Family-friendly opportunities for two-way conversations focused on building trust and honoring family insight and knowledge.	A variety of written documents (newsletters, flyers), automated alerts, or quick student/parent updates about academic progress.
Periodic celebrations focused on highlighting parent/educator/ student collaboration successes and teamwork.	Weekly, monthly, or annual presentations or updates about school compliance, progress, or plans.

The Collective Brainstorm

Now that you have had a chance to go through each of the questions and scenarios that align with the four recommendations, you should feel more familiar with how the five practices can be integrated to help you create an authentic and improved approach to reaching families that have not yet been reached.

Review the brainstorm solutions you collectively developed with the parents and colleagues you selected to help broaden your perspective. Integrate those solutions in the "Authentic & Improved Practice" summary chart that follows. Continue filling out the chart by reflecting on your Authentic Partnership Self-Assessment, the lessons you've learned, and the relevant tips and strategies from each section. Be sure to refer to the beginning of the book where you listed some of the factors that personally make you want to engage in a project or partnership. Including some of the descriptors you used to identify your motivation and engagement preferences will help provide additional details for your summary chart.

The last section of this chart—Authentic and Improved Strategy or Approach—is the synthesis of all of your conversations, learning, and outreach over the course of completing this guide. By this point, you may have already utilized some of the new strategies you list; by collaborating on the completion of this guide with parents and colleagues, you have already taken an enormous first step in the creation of an authentic school–community partnership.

Authentic & Improved Practice Summary Chart				
	Earn Trust Early	Share Responsibility Intentionally	Balance Expectations Transparently	Measure Efforts Meaningfully
Brainstorm Solution Summary From Each Section				
Authentic Partnership Practice(s) That Will Be Used				
New Learning Collected From this Guide				
Authentic and Improved Strategy or Approach				

Once you've completed your chart, you are an excellent candidate for facilitating or leading the school team portion at the end of each of the recommendation sections of this workbook. You'll be equipped to encourage your peers to engage in the critical conversations necessary to develop effective schoolwide practices and reach unreached families for equity and student achievement.

The Next Steps

Now that you've listed the authentic and improved ideas and approaches you've developed as a result of going through the workbook, decide how you will implement and share your improved ideas and approaches with others. Think about school or planning meetings that are already scheduled, as well as new opportunities you can create to share your new learning. As you integrate the approaches, make sure you are intentional about explaining and laying the groundwork needed to embed the Four Equity Partnership Recommendations and the Five Authentic Leadership Practices schoolwide.

Pay special attention to the importance of including the voice of the parents and colleagues with whom you worked as well as including new parent voices to implement your new approach with consistency, integrity, and credibility. You should notice and celebrate improvements in student engagement and an increase in the number of positive interactions between staff and families as you apply the recommendations and practices schoolwide and year round.

Educators who complete this workbook and apply their authentic and improved approaches with success will serve as ideal candidates for leading or facilitating discussions linked to supporting their colleagues or schoolwide implementation of authentic and improved approaches.

When schools prioritize earning parents' trust early, sharing responsibility intentionally, balancing expectations transparently, and measuring efforts meaningfully, it provides a platform for effective partnerships and authentic engagement. As more educators in your school begin to understand the value of connecting with families to celebrate and learn about their students' cultural assets and norms, they will also be able to help establish increased engagement levels for all students, making it more likely that they and their colleagues will reach families that they've not yet reached for equity and student achievement.

Appendix

WHAT YOU WANT TO KNOW BUT MAY BE AFRAID TO ASK

Some educators have questions that have not been answered in the previous sections of this workbook. A list of questions that tend to come up in circles where educators have not yet gained confidence about the positive impact that comes from engaging families for equity and student achievement follows.

Read the short answers provided under each of the questions, then come up with your own answers to each of the questions. Understanding the perspective and misunderstandings that exist for some of your colleagues will help you respond to the pushback and prepare you to create a more effective and authentic approach as you work to implement your strategies for reaching the families you've not yet reached in your effort to improve student outcomes.

1 Why do educators have to be the first to initiate the partnership connection? If parents know their child best, shouldn't they be the one to start the conversation?

Yes, and while parents usually have the confidence that they know their child best, they typically do not always have that same level of confidence when it comes to knowing the rules and expectations set by schools and educators. In most cases, parents who have not been reached view educators and building leaders as the host of the school and they often see themselves as uninvited or unwanted guests. Guests usually feel more comfortable visiting, when they can confirm that the host sincerely wants them there.

2 If traditional communication methods work for most parents in the school, why should extra efforts be made to reach small groups who may not believe in being involved in their child's education?

If students are not performing well and the families of those students have not been reached, you run the risk of losing the opportunity to help the student(s) succeed if you have not tried to reach the parent/family in a method that is effective for them or their child/teenager.

3 Educators' jobs require them to teach students effectively. Why should so much attention go toward trying to be effective at reaching parents?

No matter how effective educators feel they are with their curriculum delivery or instructional skills, developing authentic partnerships with families makes it more likely that teachers will be able to work smarter rather than harder to engage and motivate students as learners.

4 If parents aren't already involved, isn't it best just to keep it that way to prevent unnecessary complications?

Avoiding or delaying parent interactions and partnerships increases the chance that the unintended connection will be initiated by the family or the student. If the first connection is created by a misunderstanding or conflict, it will take longer to resolve the issue or build trust than if the conversation had been initiated by the educator for a positive purpose.

5 Isn't it unreasonable to expect families to want to be engaged in cases where there is a language barrier, limited education, or overwhelming economic pressures?

Giving parents opportunities to be involved as partners is a requirement connected to Title I and Every Student Succeeds Act guidelines. These guidelines also require that important information be provided in the parents' first language. Most families want their child's circumstances to improve beyond what they can provide regardless of their income, culture, language, or economic background. Engaging families as partners helps ensure that each child has access to the opportunities that support their ability to become contributing members of society.

6 How do we address the problem regarding parents who forget to update their contact information?

When parents forget to update their contact information, try to contact someone on the relatives/emergency list and ask if they can have the parent contact you. If there are no emergency names listed on the contact list and the parent's email address and phone numbers are both inaccurate, try mailing a postcard requesting the parent call the school to provide updated information. If the address isn't current, ask the student to have their parent contact you. If none of these options work, as a *last resort try reaching them on their work number to ask if they can provide updated contact information. *In some instances, getting calls from their child's school can create added stress at work.

7 What about parents who don't want to be involved?

Like educators, most parents enjoy being around people who appreciate what they have to offer and make them feel welcome, especially if those people are trustworthy, respectful, and care about their children. It's unusual for parents to choose not to be involved in schools that make an honest effort to develop authentic partnerships and consistently address the barriers they face with transportation, language, and/or scheduling conflicts.

8 What if all of these practices work and we end up having more engagement than we're prepared to address?

If you've developed an authentic approach to family partnerships with a focus on building trust, sharing responsibility, and balancing expectations for both educators and families, you will be able to have honest and transparent conversations about how to establish and sustain balance throughout the partnership.

9 How can teachers find the time or gain the experience needed to implement all or even some of these strategies effectively?

Building trust doesn't require special training or technical skills that can be taught. Parents typically give educators the benefit of the doubt and positive kudos just for trying to be more effective at reaching them in an effort to promote success and support for their child. As long as the efforts are grounded in the concepts linked to the Four Equity Partnership Recommendations (building trust early, sharing responsibility intentionally, balancing expectations transparently, and measuring efforts meaningfully), none of the outcomes will be implemented in isolation, so you won't be the only person responsible for success or flaws. An authentic and effective approach doesn't require complex new strategies or adding more events and activities. It actually gives educators and families the opportunity to communicate more effectively on the front end. It can also help reduce conflicts, which saves time and reduces the number of meetings needed to address misunderstandings .

10 What if I use the recommendations or practices incorrectly and instead of engaging families for equity and student achievement, I end up offending parents?

Most parents can tell the difference between strategic tactics designed to manipulate them into doing what schools want and genuine efforts focused on building trust and authentic partnerships. The latter is usually applauded, even if implementation is a little clumsy.

REFERENCES

Hammond, Z. (2015). *Culturally responsive teaching & the brain: Promoting authentic engagement and rigor among culturally and linguistically diverse students.* Thousand Oaks, CA: Corwin.

Hattie, J. A. C. (2009). *Visible learning: A synthesis of over 800 meta-analyses relating to achievement.* Abingdon, UK: Routledge.

Mapp, K. L., & Kuttner, P. J. (2013). *Partners in education: A dual capacity-building framework for family–school partnerships.* Austin, TX: SEDL, U.S. Department of Education. Retrieved from https://www2.ed.gov /documents/family-community/partners-education.pdf

CPSIA information can be obtained
at www.ICGtesting.com
Printed in the USA
BVHW081407270720
584784BV00005B/180